LEARN HOW **9 ROOKIE CEOs** GOT THERE,
EXECUTED, CREATED THEIR STORIES, AND LED!

THE ROOKIE CEO

YOU CAN'T MAKE THIS STUFF UP!

BILL MILLER

Foreword by **RICH TEHRANI**

Published by Beelinebill Publishing

Cover Design by 99Designs and cover image is modified stock illustration ID: 183282761 under license from Shutterstock.com.

For more information, email bill@billmillertheauthor.com

ISBN: Paperback 978-1-7356538-1-5
ISBN: eBook 978-1-7356538-0-8
ISBN: Hard Cover 978-1-7356538-2-2

For my fiancée, Connie Lund, who has provided
me heartfelt love and support!

For the CEOs who worked with me in the many companies
where they provided material for all the stories in the book

You must learn from the mistakes
of others. You can't possibly live long
enough to make them all yourself.

—Sam Levinson

FREE OFFER

As a thank you for purchasing my book, I am offering a free Rookie CEO Guide by emailing me at bill@billmillertheCEOguy.com where you will receive a free copy of "Top 7 Tips for the Rookie CEO" that you can't find anywhere else!

These valuable tips come from my experiences reporting to the 9 featured rookie CEOs in this book that will fuel your new CEO role when these or similar bumps in the road hit you head on!

TABLE OF CONTENTS

FOREWORD

Why do 90 percent of companies fail? What are the ingredients of a successful organization? Why do companies starting at roughly the same time, with similar solutions, have vastly different growth rates, fundraising success, and customer acquisition rates?

An immense amount of capital is wasted in failed startups, not to mention wasted dreams and wasted potential. According to the SBA, nearly 600 thousand businesses fail in a typical year. Assuming each represents $200 thousand in wasted capital allocation, this amounts to $120 billion wasted each year.

I am CEO of TMC, tmcnet.com, a tech, media, and conference company, and in this capacity, I have met with over 10 thousand CEOs in my career. What always fascinates me is how the personality, passion, enthusiasm, management style, and values of the CEO can help make or break an organization.

I met the author of this book, Bill Miller, around two decades ago, when he was hired at a company that became a customer and later a partner of TMC. We became friends, and what never ceased to amaze me was Bill's insight into the industry and the personalities all around us. His experience is vast—spanning from established companies to startups. He spent a long time in the open-source community, which is inherently different from a traditional commercial organization.

During this journey, he learned the sort of management styles and managers that are successful. Often, he would predict to me in advance what would happen to people and companies in the market, and he was generally right.

People are like snowflakes, everyone is unique. But still, each is made of water, and they can be categorized by size, temperature, shape, and texture. In other words, snowflakes and people can be placed in categories to some degree, allowing us to get a sense of what we are dealing with. Some snow is great for making snowballs, and some people are great for leading companies.

What you will learn from this book is which types of people are the ones that will help make an organization successful. What behaviors cross the line. What activities often result in subpar execution and what inclusive and successful leadership looks like.

It is a great read for investors, entrepreneurs, and people with an interest in business or technology. It is a solid perspective on how some great tech companies were built and a behind-the-scenes account of corporate America from the largest companies to the smallest startups.

At one of our ITEXPO conferences, we were fortunate enough to have John Sculley as one of our keynoters, and he shared the story of how the board at Apple replaced Steve Jobs with him. Steve had a difficult personality, as John explained. He admitted to what we all know now, it was a mistake to fire Steve.

Apple languished for years as a result.

For decades after this mistake, tech investors have seen the value in keeping their founders, with warts and all, at the head of their organizations. Investors took this to the limit allowing WeWork founder, Adam Neumann, to make a lot of errors, which were the result of poor corporate governance controls. As a result of this mess, investors have been reminded that even founders need to be let go from time to time and that acting on early red flags can save a lot of pain in the future. WeWork ended up giving Softbank's Vision Fund a loss of $17.7 billion as of this writing.

People matter. Personalities matter. This book is a great guide on what does and does not work when looking to fund, start, or work for a successful organization. I hope it helps you get to and stay in the coveted 10 percent of business success stories.

Rich Tehrani
CEO
TMC

INTRODUCTION

The Making of a CEO

CEOs are unique personas and the face of their companies and employees. CEOs are powerful. Their management team and employees respond to them, often dropping everything regardless of whether the CEO was thinking out loud or actually directing them to execute an action. In some situations, the rookie CEO does not realize or is not aware of this power and how it affects people. This new power of the CEO can kill or slow down projects that may be critical success factors for the company they are now leading. Of course, the rookie may choose to kill a project that is floundering and reallocate the budget to new projects, but that's not what I'm referring to here.

In some companies, the employees and executives don't push back because they want to help the new CEO and respond with actions, not questions. In reality, the CEO needs people who challenge them and ask as many questions as they can to gain an interlock on the actions. I have seen this miscommunication occur over and over again. Typically, the results are not pretty unless there is clarity for everyone involved. CEOs carry a big stick, and oftentimes they don't think about that.

It is important to understand that a rookie CEO can come from any cultural or business background. To be hired, a rookie CEO gets their new role after rigorous interviewing, passing of various tests, and earning the position. If it's a startup, they are entrepreneurial by nature and either started the company or were hired by a founder, an investor, or the board of directors. The new CEO role may be a natural progression for them, or they may be jumping right in. Some people may be leaving a cushy job for the rookie CEO role while some have been planning for years and it's time to take the leap. Regardless, actual stories—which you'll find in this book—can provide a variety of data points and entertainment along the way to the rookie CEO pedestal.

My experience-rich executive career included reporting directly to nine CEOs, for over two decades in six companies, all of whom turned out to be rookies, meaning first-time CEOs, in their roles. Some, who were new to the role, were not yet set in their leadership ways, and some, who were a few years into their rookie stints, were established in their leadership style and business processes.

My intent with this book is to prepare and fuel future CEOs, open the eyes of existing CEOs and executives who report to them, and entertain readers with some head-turning and educational true stories. In today's world, the barrier to start new companies can be relatively low, and inexperienced people will become rookie CEOs when they start their new companies. This book is a resource for the new kid on the CEO block to have a snapshot into nine real scenarios to prepare their mindset to transition into the new role smoothly, to prevent costly mistakes, and to consider their methodologies as they dig in. Think of it as a GPS for the rookie CEO.

I have had a goal of publishing this book for well over a decade and have been preparing for it by collecting information and stories, observing, and many times in deep discussions and debates with these nine rookie CEOs, as I learned what made these folks tick. I am excited to share these true, most intriguing, and crazy experiences. As well as the important takeaways.

Just so you can more explicitly understand my background: I started as a software engineer and progressed into these roles: sales engineer, product marketing, and product manager. My titles over the past two decades when I reported to the featured rookie CEOs include VP of product management and marketing, VP of marketing, VP of product management, VP of operations, VP of strategic planning and alliance management, and VP of broadband services. Since 2011, I've also worked as a consultant, guiding CEOs (some whom I mention in this book) to become the best they can be. If you are interested in exploring the possibility of working together, please contact me: bill@billmillertheCEOguy.com.

Our 9 Featured Rookies

A rookie CEO's story provides insight as to how they will lead their new company. As already stated, CEOs can come from anywhere, and I will share stories of nine different rookie CEOs, so you'll see how a CEO's background has a direct effect on the culture that emerges in the company, the working environment for employees, and other key aspects of the company.

These stories are certified true by me from my perspective, but the names are fictional. We cover over two decades of my direct personal experiences, which includes women and men rookie CEOs, startup CEOs, and those who were in their first CEO role and had been in the role for several years. The latter rookie CEOs already were running their companies for some time and might have been reinventing, restructuring, or scaling them. These are the nine featured rookies you'll read more about in this book:

- *The Builder*: engineering background and a founder rookie CEO of a startup; replaced by the Dealmaker
- *The Dealmaker*: sales background and rookie CEO of a startup

- *The Innovatist*: engineering background, former product manager, former general manager, and a founder rookie CEO of a startup
- *The Cyclone*: engineering background, former general manager and rookie CEO of a large-stage
- *The Pipeline*: sales background and rookie CEO of a large-stage
- *The Technoid*: engineering background and founder rookie CEO of a startup
- *The Flyboy:* student and engineering background, and founder rookie CEO of a mid-revenue; replaced by the General
- *The General*: operations background, former general manager and rookie CEO of a mid-revenue
- *The Opportunist*: research background and rookie CEO of a mid-revenue

Their varied backgrounds play well into our analysis of their strengths, challenges, and learning curves.

Many of the featured rookie CEOs started their companies with friends or they hired friends or former colleagues, who, in turn, brought in their friends and former colleagues, which by nature should create a tree of trust. Generally, this concept works most of the time. The team needs to have the right people in the right job regardless if it's a startup or established multinational corporation. This can be a daunting task for the rookie CEO.

If the rookie CEO role is in an established company, their awareness of their new-found power kicks in day one, but it may be invisible to the rookie. If they start off the wrong way, recovery may be elusive for some period of time. People talk and compare notes all the time. Employees will decide on their own how the new CEO will shake things up, and every day from the get-go this will continue. Typically, there will be a lot of movement over the rookie CEO's first three to six months. People, teams, projects, and company structure may change once the rookie gets their footing and pulls the trigger.

The management team may learn quickly, or over the first few weeks from the team meetings and their one-on-one meetings, the direction the rookie CEO will be taking the company in. This includes reorganizations, restructures, and headcount cuts or adds. The rookie may decide on a different direction for the company than what they inherited if this is an established company. Maybe the direction requires a complete make-over. The rookie CEO may already be planning which trusted friends and former colleagues will be coming in and which executives they will be replacing.

The Contours of This Book

I have created what I call the "PPLC" framework to provide a unique structured perspective into how a rookie CEO leads their company:

- P = Path to CEO
- P = Philosophy
- L = Leadership Style
- C = Culture

This book's four sections will correlate with the PPLC framework as follows:

P = Section 1—Path to CEO

You will see how the paths taken to the CEO role can have an impact on how the CEO gets to their new pedestal. Why is this so important? The rookie will not let go of their passion that got them promoted or fast-tracked and their approach to leading. Sometimes, they may become disillusioned as they learn what they have gotten into. This drives immediate action from the rookie to modify their initial thinking. For example, will the rookie attend every meeting possible? From hardware, software, and service design, to product launch and website, the rookie by nature wants to be involved in every way. How will this style affect the operation of the company and its success? Will the rookie direct key team members on what to do and how to do it? Or is their communication style well-rounded where the rookie is learning and asks excellent "have you considered" questions?

P = Section 2—CEO Philosophy

In this section, we look at rookie CEOs' philosophies that drive the core values and principles of how their companies operate under normal conditions. Some examples include: how will meetings be conducted? How is information shared: is it an open- or closed-communication of information approach or a need-to-know type of philosophy? How are budgets created, managed, and tracked? Does the rookie like to keep certain things mysterious, or is everything (for the most part) open?

L = Section 3—Leadership

This section focuses on the CEO's style of leadership and what day-to-day life will look like for everyone. What does the rookie CEO stand for? What is their operating style? Does the rookie want to quietly grow the company, securing multiple customers before doing widespread public relations? Or does the rookie want to make a big public relations splash? I have experienced both styles. It depends on the leadership style the rookie brings. Is the rookie a controlling leader? Do they have an ego that may be difficult to deal with? Does the leader have integrity? I have some historical data points to share that may enlighten some readers. Although every rookie CEO will have earned their new position because they have integrity at the highest interview levels, oftentimes we find out that this is not true in daily operations. Is the rookie a planner or seat-of-the-pants type who operates "ready-fire-aim" style? There is a time and place for different styles. Understanding leadership styles and how they impact company success is the focus of this section.

C = Section 4—Culture

Some companies take culture very seriously. Well-known companies like Zappos, Disney, the New England Patriots, HubSpot, and IBM have historic well-known culture codes, and people that don't fit the culture don't get hired or don't stay at the company long. In established companies, some rookies take time and energy to learn more about the breadth of culture and over time refine or change it through actions. Startup CEOs create a culture from day one that begins to emerge based on their PPL (i.e., their path to leadership, philosophy, and leadership style). Do groups help each other? Do people work in fear? Are there group-style lunches or sessions that encourage participation? How is conflict resolved? How are customers treated? Because customer service is often a differentiator for a company, do people get educated in delivering top-notch service? An example is the Cyclone who brought "red carpet service" to the company, which was not exactly what was inherited by this rookie. The Cyclone's definition of "red carpet service" was to mirror customer service from a particular major airline company's playbook, but in the business-to-business environment rather than the business-to-consumer market.

The rookie CEO brings a culture based on their philosophies and leadership styles. The results will be driven from their individual PPLC, which is the core of the book. Just knowing how PPLC works together will better prepare the new CEO to be aware of and smoothly enter a new role, or start their company as the CEO founder. Accordingly, I have assembled my personal perspectives and created this PPLC framework for soon-to-be or newly minted CEOs to use to prepare and fuel themselves for a strong start and highly successful finish.

And so we turn to the first P in the PPLC framework—Path to CEO—in section 1 of this book.

SECTION 1
PATH TO CEO

We are what we repeatedly do. Excellence,
then, is not an act, but a habit.

—Aristotle

CHAPTER 1

Background

The CEO brings with them their unique background, which forms the foundation of their entire persona, the foundation on which the other attributes are layered. The first P of PPLC is the CEO's "Path to CEO," which is unique based on their background.

Their individual background brings with it the experience level of the rookie; their vision and passion, which may be financial, product-related, or technical from the development perspective; their preferred approach, whether confrontational or collaborative; their preferred methods to build out their team; their approach to budgeting and planning; the outside influencers of the rookie; and their PLCs, meaning their philosophy, leadership, and culture.

Of the nine CEOs featured, we have three former general managers, all of whom started their careers as engineers; two of whom were sales executives; three came from research and development; one from operations; and one from pure research. Two were founder CEOs who were replaced by other rookie CEOs. This type of move, replacing a rookie CEO with another rookie CEO, brings with it an entire new set of challenges, such as extreme PPLC-driven changes of different philosophies and styles.

Stage of Company and Background of CEO

Another factor to consider is the stage of the company with the type of CEO needed to lead the company. Retained CEO recruiting firms provide guidance and attributes of CEOs by company stage, where this book discusses my actual experiences based on my observations and analysis using my PPLC framework. Please note that all stages require the ability to manage the board of directors.

For reference, this is my view of the stages of a technology company, with each stage requiring a different type of leadership, as follows:

Early-Stage Startup ($0–$5M)—fundraiser, technically savvy and solid basic business understanding, ability to sell the new technology to investors and beachhead customers (meaning "building relationships" and selling), and ability to build the startup team.

Early-Revenue Growth (post $5M)—company needs to scale to $10M or higher, needs a leader who is not involved in every detail and has a trusted leadership team that does their jobs. Their regular meetings discuss challenges, priorities, and sales opportunities. Begin implementing processes and business systems that will scale to the next level, but are simplified for ease of managing. The CEO may be raising additional capital to continue growth and move to the next level.

Mid-Revenue Growth ($10M–$30M)—requires the ability to scale sales channels and create infrastructure and support for the company. A focus on growth programs, process, and continued relationships with investors and beachhead customers. By this time, details for running the company come together usually by a chief operating officer, and the company may be structured for scale depending on what the customer profile looks like and sales/support model becomes. The CEO may be raising additional capital to scale the mid-sized company.

High-Growth ($30–$100M)—requires a leader who spends all their time on the big picture in terms of sales channels, models, and services. The focus on margins and investments required to get to this growth level is different than "just get it done" in the previous stages.

Large-Stage Company or Division of Larger Company (over $100M)—requires a totally different focus for the CEO now: big picture, global infrastructure, leading a diverse employee base, and being the face of the company. An experienced executive team runs and operates their division or business functions while the CEO leads and drives strategic direction.

To be clear, there are people that can move through these stages as they learn and who are always self-improving and have the highest level of success. These leaders do not require any specific education either (just because they have a Harvard MBA does not translate into the most successful leader). For example, Mark Zuckerberg, Bill Gates, and Michael Dell grew their companies through the stages with no college degree—they were college dropouts, but they are entrepreneurs. The makeup of these individuals is unique in that they hired great people onto their team at the right time as they grew. They worked together, structured properly, and prioritized properly, with the CEO leading the way.

Overview of Our Nine Rookies

Let's take a moment to look at the nine featured CEOs to get a general overview of them, their backgrounds, and how that aligned with the companies, in terms of size and stage, that they became rookie CEOs of.

The Builder: this serial entrepreneur was a startup founder and CEO with a solid engineering background. Her co-founder had been with her previously as they had exited twice (sold their company) and together convinced me to join this company with an 18-month exit strategy, which was very enticing, with tier one venture capital firms funding the Builder and her team. I joined this company early on and found the Builder to be a terrific person, without a bad bone in her body. She was trusting, extremely bright, and had a mild-mannered demeanor. Most of the Builder's hires were people she already knew. I was one she did not know, but she was introduced to me by a venture capitalist. Hiring outside of her circle of friends was one of the Builder's biggest challenges.

The Dealmaker: hired into the Builder's company as vice president of sales, he was promoted to CEO because of his ability to sell the board of directors and founder CEO, and his outstanding presentation skills. A big deal kind of guy, he loved to talk to customers and partners, and was always selling and throwing out hypothetical scenarios to generate inspiring discussions. It was his style. A believer in spending to move sales ahead, he was a marketing VP's (i.e., me) hero because he could see the return on investment of various marketing programs. The Dealmaker was outgoing, trusting, and loud. Future rookies will see how his approach to trust got him into trouble with a hire he made to fill a gap in his skillset, which comes up in a later discussion on signature authority. Later, you'll read my absolute favorite rookie CEO story starring the Dealmaker that's called "The Wheelbarrow."

The Innovatist: this rookie's background was in engineering, product management, and general management progressively. He always had a technical angle because it was his passion. Over his rookie stint, he had moments of brilliance and incredible tenacity while working very closely with the private investors. He did build this company from square one with his first three hires in a small town, equipped with a folding table and chairs from Costco. It truly was a low budget startup. His philosophy was what shaped the environment, and the private investors' role shaped the results. This rookie had a vision I loved and bought into, but the investors shut down the initial vision because they were inexperienced, did not understand, did not listen (even though we had a lead customer installed and operating), and the investors were very influential because it was their money. We had no company without their investment and for that we were thankful, but it was a challenge creating innovative products and marketing and selling via channels the investors did not understand so well. The Innovatist worked relentlessly to overcome the challenge to deliver top-tier customers.

The original vision of the Innovatist was to change the world with an innovative new product idea. It is typical to find innovation such as this from a small startup, which has the ability to disrupt an existing market. The rookie did his best to accomplish this feat in spite of the investors and his limited CEO experience. He led the charge to pivot and make something out of the original vision going forward. This rookie hired many trusted friends, but when things got challenging, he did not like confrontation, and it caused him much stress. It's something to think about and expect for future rookie CEOs.

The Cyclone: this rookie CEO came from a technical role early in her career, advanced nicely to general manager of a large public corporation, and was a pioneer in delivering the dotcom ecosystem. When the Cyclone was introduced to the organization at a national sales meeting, many people were surprised and, in the case of my colleagues, alarmed and worried from day one. For me, personally, I am open to change, so initially I did not have any issues with the Cyclone, except I had a new boss, which always brings some level of hope accompanied by nervousness and angst. This rookie brought to the party a controlling style, a huge ego, and during her tenure at the company, she was very misguided (look for one of my favorite stories coming up about the "Seven Dwarfs"). A former general manager, this rookie understood all elements of running a business and knew how to attack underperforming business areas with a vengeance. The challenge was how do you execute when you have to earn the trust and respect of an inherited broad range of people? Although at times The Cyclone overcommunicated, if she'd instituted better planning with clear goals and more optimized communication, she would have eliminated some difficult situations the leadership team needed to deal with.

The Pipeline: this short-term rookie has a small role here, in that he became an interim CEO for a short time. I was hired by a seasoned veteran CEO only to find out on my first day of the new job that the veteran who'd hired me was fired. Alarming, yes, but the Pipeline had been involved in the interview process and had voted me on to the island and had a vested interest as the then senior vice president of sales. This rookie's newfound power was focused only on sales, so he needed to be surrounded by all the subject matter experts. As life was about golf, his deals were done over 18 holes at a top-tier golf course. I took golf lessons just to keep up with the foursomes we had in business meetings.

The Technoid: the Technoid was a former engineer whose company was acquired, and she did not stay with the acquirer. A subject matter technical expert, I met her giving a 30-second pitch to investors at a networking event, a pitch that left a lot to be desired. After meeting for coffee, we teamed up for over a year while raising money and developing new products. A quiet and introverted person, the Technoid really was a pure techie trying to build a company from an innovative and simple idea. We worked from our homes, she brought her team of engineers who also worked from home, and we got all the way to term sheet signing day with a venture capital firm and a technology strategic investor. On the signing day, we were told by the strategic investor that in spite of the fact they loved what we were doing, it would cost twice as much and take twice as long as we projected, and they decided to go in another direction. We dismantled the startup after that event, as all investors we spoke with had required that same particular strategic investor or they were not interested. The Technoid was intelligent and quiet. She recognized the need to add business-side talent to round out her startup management team. From her story future CEOs should consider the type of talent their leadership team needs to build and grow their company.

The Flyboy: one of the most interesting of the rookie CEOs, the Flyboy created a company while a student in college with no money, found his early employees on campus, found a corporate investor, and built a profitable company just by hiring trusted friends and using advisors prior to my arrival. He was brilliant, caring, compassionate, and engaging. The Flyboy built a company that valued younger folks and their potential for growth and learning. He had a culture unlike any other in the region where we were located or, for that matter, technology companies in general. The Flyboy loved to have "themed" days, something the employees loved to participate in! I was introduced to this company and Flyboy by a tier one venture capitalist who was investing a significant amount of cash, and he wanted an experienced executive to help guide the company with the Flyboy. I always felt fortunate to land this role at this company and get to know the Flyboy. He was fun, creative, open, and trusting. He hired inexperienced people and educated and trained them in the exciting culture he built. The Flyboy did control spending, but once I joined, he was able to trust me to own my own functions and decisions. I used to tell the Flyboy, "There is no box," in his thought process because he was always thinking "outside the box," and he had no limits or boundaries. The Flyboy's new passion is aviation, which he was introduced to in the General's plane when we flew one time to a partner location. He would not give the mic controls back to the General once he got it in his hands talking to air traffic control. He was featured on the cover of several publications and received notoriety from his efforts and success at his company.

The General: the General was one of two of the Flyboy's trusted advisors and was on our board of directors because his public company was a corporate investor. He became CEO and the Flyboy remained chairman of the board. The General was a solid executive coming from a large public company, running operations for one of two business units. His background was from product development and engineering, and he understood all major business functions pretty well. He did have to learn some new software technology trends and business challenges, but was up to the task. He was the most well-rounded and polished executive as a rookie CEO. He brought his VP of sales with him on day one, so he did not have to wait a year after leaving his company to recruit. The culture Flyboy had built changed completely under the General. The business pivoted, decisions and processes were different, and everything was tracked in dashboards.

The Opportunist: the Opportunist had been a startup CEO about 13 years before I joined and was still CEO, but the company had plateaued and his vision was to grow by at least doubling the revenues. His original vision, which he had achieved, was helping individuals—one-person companies—have a phone system very much like large global companies even if they have no technical skills. Customers could have an 800 number with all the big company phone system features and messaging. He brought in a small team that combined open source software with new special purpose software and built his company. He later expanded into small business systems, and I joined him first as a consultant, then full-time and helped his cause. Along the way, the Opportunist utilized a CEO peer group to help him learn as he grew. One of his management team members defined him as "opportunistic, driven, and eager." He was reinventing the company moving forward.

Communication with his leadership team was his biggest hurdle, combining his level of intelligence with a lack of ability of most of his team to communicate clearly. This shines a light on learning experiences for many bright executives. In meetings, the Opportunist would direct a manager to do something. All but one of his management team would never ask clarification questions. The engineering leader would typically ask three questions in order to get interlock and clarity with this rookie on what he was asking them to do. In the next meeting, those who never got clarity would not achieve the original request, which would be upsetting to the Opportunist. Between his CEO peer group coaching and my feedback to him, his communication with the team improved greatly.

This rookie hired an incredible human resources consultant that worked with us to help install a new process to build an "A-player" team. With this consultant's process and their working relationship with the Opportunist, we hired a team of top A-player talent, restructured the company, and set the company up for acquisition by a company that led to a flourishing future for him and the team.

Stages of Companies and Our Featured Rookies

The nine featured CEOs in this book came to their respective companies in the following stages:

- Three startups—all early-stage pre-revenue
- Two established companies that grew to current revenue stage (both were in the mid-revenue growth stage, ranging from $9M to $15M in revenue) and still under the original founder CEO
- One large-stage global multinational company, >$40B, with division revenues of $250M

Startup CEO

There are three rookie CEOs that fall into the startup CEO category: the Builder, the Technoid, and the Innovatist. The Builder was a serial entrepreneur who had exited but not as a CEO. Her background was in development at a large, successful public company. She was brilliant as an engineer. Her approach to everything was on the technical side. However, like any successful startup CEO, the Builder was great at positioning her new company and selling the technology. She got the role because venture capitalists asked her to build a product family and gave her series A funding. Later, she hired the Dealmaker as VP of sales, who, next, ended up as the new rookie CEO and the Builder moved to chief strategy officer and VP of engineering. The Dealmaker was the consummate sales executive who is featured in a few stories coming up later.

The Technoid, also a first-time CEO, had formerly been a technical director on new technology that had been acquired by a larger company. We met over coffee at a restaurant, and we were off to raise venture capital. Her technical background was her passion and focus. We were early to market with her solution.

The Innovatist was the only featured rookie CEO who'd left a large public company to start his own company. He was able to secure private financing and maintained the investor relationship close to the vest for the entire time, which caused some challenges for him and the team that he built. Being a former engineer and product manager, he was very technical and was involved in every aspect of the company from selecting product architecture, design, to component selection, and more. His passion and enthusiasm were second to none. His challenge was the board of directors.

Mid-Revenue CEO

There were two rookies in the mid-revenue growth stage class of CEO: the Flyboy and the Opportunist. Both started their companies, in fact in the same year, but one, the Flyboy, was a student at college and very technical, and the other, the Opportunist, was self-employed trying to find a business venture that he'd stumbled upon. Each of these companies were about 50 to 60 people in size with about $9M to $15M in revenue. Both were profitable but lacked some key roles to scale their companies or get acquired. Neither company previously had VPs, but both committed to me as a VP. I was a consultant at both companies before being hired full-time.

The Flyboy was a college student when he started his company. He found his team via the school network. He was able to secure funding from a corporation and the rest was history. He built a leader in their market space without "adult supervision" for his company. When he raised venture funds, I entered the picture. He was personable, smart as hell, and fun. To take the company to the next level, the Flyboy hired the General, a former public company COO, as the new rookie

CEO—my second rookie CEO at this company. The General was very different. Day one, he brought his VP of sales over and also told me my role would be split a year later. A former engineer and proven operations executive and board member, he was a seasoned executive but a rookie CEO. The company was acquired under his leadership.

The Opportunist was from a different market, but he ended up starting a company and leading and learning a totally new business that nicely filled a market gap. As his company grew, he promoted others until they hit their ceiling and then he wanted to remove them, but it was hard as their kids had grown up together. During the workday, he mostly focused on his work in his office except for meetings and rarely was walking around talking to his staff, at least when I was there. His style of talking to people was through regular all-employee meetings and events, with dinner and drinks with spouses and significant others often at local restaurants after hours.

Large-Stage CEO

This large-company experience was unlike any other. The Cyclone came from a global public company and held a general management role there. The company I was at had a huge leadership hole as the CEO who'd hired me left between my acceptance of the position and my start date. As a large-company rookie CEO, the Cyclone brought the large-company mindset. Spending lots of cash on projects that did little to nothing to create revenue—it was a sandbox with several cronies brought in to run groups they had no ideas about. It was sad for the company in many ways. This rookie was the inspiration for this book because of the bizarre things she did, such as try to invest millions of dollars in a new partner that was a past colleague that made no sense for our company—no product-market fit—but this move did show the Cyclone's willingness to take risks. This rookie's goal was to acquire these former colleagues, and their executive team would replace our executive team at the time. This was unknown to our team at the time.

The Cyclone's previous GM role was preceded by engineering and systems engineering roles. At large companies, the CEO is several levels removed from technology and only looks at numbers and very high-level presentations, so when she presented information in this manner to lower-level employees, they found it confusing.

Rookie CEO Story: The Bonus That Wasn't

Imagine you just received your hard-earned bonus check, direct deposit. The Cyclone called a senior leadership team meeting to ask all executives to allow the company to remove this direct deposit back from everyone's checking accounts to cover company cash flow shortfalls that the team was unaware of. *Poof*—gone. All of it.

Poor planning on the Cyclone's part caused an emergency on the senior leadership team's part. That was a sad day for the team who had earned their bonuses!

As a guideline for future CEOs, cash flow can become an issue depending on how you are funded, your revenue stage, the length of your customer payment cycles, or for some other reason. Rookie CEOs should consider the possibility that this can happen and how they might handle the situation. Because the Cyclone's path to becoming a CEO didn't include this kind of experience, and she never pursued any advisors in this area, she resorted to the above and-poof-it-is-gone takeback!

Rookie CEO Story: Pajama Day

To end this chapter on a fun note, let's turn to the Flyboy: the Flyboy loved to have fun as part of the company culture and on occasion would have a themed day. This particular one was "PJ day." On this day, there was a training class consisting of global software people, and since he was CEO, the Flyboy spoke in front of the class in "shorty" PJs. I found myself wondering if it was fun, surreal, or liberating for these software folks from all over the world—India, the United Kingdom, the Czech Republic, Italy, Hong Kong, etc.—to see this leader of a $20M company in this get-up. Indeed, you can't make this stuff up!

Even if such a themed day doesn't naturally fall in your repertoire based on your background, these types of themed days can be very much fun for all. Think about how you can create something unique and memorable, such as crazy t-shirt day, crazy hat day, ugly sweater day, anything that can generate participation and fun for the employees and management team.

Staff appreciation day

Chapter 1 Takeaways

- Whatever your background is, you can become a rookie CEO. *no*
- Study the behavior and activities of CEOs, and model your personal style and behavior around what you want to be.
- Think about your own PPLC: your path to CEO, your philosophy, your leadership style, and your approach to culture. As you work in different companies, study these aspects, and you will see patterns that emerge and that you can grow into your own.
- Behavior matters.

CHAPTER 2

Functional Expertise

A review of the functional expertise that a rookie CEO brings and how their expertise affects day-to-day strategies and behavior is a valuable exercise. It is in their former role that the rookie developed their business processes and decision-making style. The rookie CEO can come from any business function, but how they have been educated, trained, and grew in their function will drive their mindset and ultimately how they lead. Remember, a successful CEO can come from any business function. The new CEO needs a vision to change or attack the market, and to be successful once they get on board in their new role.

Engineering Background

In the technology world, engineering sets the foundation for many future CEOs. Engineers are on the front end of product development. Thus, they are held to schedules that require looking at a product's requirements and translating them into technical specifications to develop and deliver. It requires understanding the big picture, understanding how the product they are developing fits into their targeted solutions, setting key project priorities, balancing and juggling resources, and creating a minimal viable product to launch with a roadmap to bring longer life to the endeavor. Their lead customers—"beachhead" customers who drive the development and feature sets—buy into not only their initial product release but the roadmap where the company is heading. Most beachheads will modify the roadmap to benefit their application, and at the very beginning, this works. But once the company gets multiple customers and experiences obstacles, it gets a bit mucky to stay focused and deliver as promised as priorities change. Engineers address these challenges much differently than sales and marketing leaders.

Some engineers can develop hardware and software without specific requirements or plans. Some engineers can build what they think the market wants. Others bring a vision to change the game. A great example of the latter is Steve Jobs whose vision was to change the world. Jobs did not start with requirements; he simply had a vision to change the world, which he did multiple times.

Many former engineering leaders start with a whiteboard accompanied by brainstorm sessions with their trusted team. Whiteboards are the source for what you may be building in a startup. This was the case for two of my startups. The founder's vision was on a whiteboard. Sometimes, the vision is in PowerPoint and an executive summary document for raising money on the outside from investors. The Cyclone, the Builder, the Technoid, the General, the Flyboy, and the Innovatist were all former engineers. The Cyclone and the Innovatist were also general managers in larger public companies. The combinations matter in their approaches. The General was an engineer who came from operations in a public company while the Flyboy was an engineering student. Only the Opportunist, the Pipeline, and the Dealmaker were not tech engineers.

What do engineers bring to their CEO role? Because engineers are motivated by solving the technical problems their product or service addresses, they are typically involved in details of design, architecture, and feature set decisions. Of course, product-market fit is critical for success, and being in meetings that are involved with this makes sense, but not so much with selecting screws and bracket materials.

My observation is that rookie CEOs who come from engineering and enjoy this involvement should let the owners of the development lead and the rookie can ask as many detailed questions as needed as a way to be involved and satisfied with progress. This facilitates the involvement but allows the trusted team leaders to lead. It is important for rookies with technical backgrounds to stay involved but support the team leaders to maintain ownership.

Sales Background

Rookie CEOs from a sales background can be interesting leaders because they are typically extroverted and not always good administrators, and they need clarity and understanding in what motivates their team. Money motivates salespeople but does not drive other business functions in the same way. In many surveys, employees always have money in their top ten motivating factors, but not at the very top. Only sales personnel rank money at the top. Later, when you read "The Wheelbarrow," my favorite story, you will see what I mean. Generally, rookies who come from a sales background can be great for early-stage startups because finding the beachhead customers (i.e., first prospects for the solution and leading "must win at all costs" customers for a new company) are critical to their success.

Operations Background

Rookie CEOs who come from an operations background—chief operating officer (COO), not manufacturing operations—should be well suited to becoming CEOs. They have already led several functions as COO and have a unique breadth across many business functions. Of our nine rookie CEOs in this book, only the General fits this role. He came into a mid-revenue growth company of which he was already on the board of directors, so he was familiar with the business. Since the COO role typically uses dashboards and metrics to run the business, a COO-turned CEO typically brings some formality to a smaller company, which makes sense, but they need to be careful not to demand too much too fast. Otherwise, project work and the culture changes will impact business momentum.

Product Manager Background

Product managers bring another broad-based and strong foundation for a potential CEO role. Product management professionals were mini-CEOs for their product lines and, as such, learned how every aspect of product definition, development, manufacture, sales, and support drives revenues and gross margins. These all must be considered in the new rookie CEO role. Product managers usually have product-line profit-and-loss accountability, and run the product line like a company. They should have a fair amount of experience with customers. They are used to getting projects done through others that don't work for them, which is critical and transferable to a CEO role. These rookies will have a broad understanding of the business machine to create, build, test, promote, and deliver to customers.

Rookie CEO Story: The Pipeline Deal That Wasn't

The Pipeline was trying to convince me there was this "deal" with an entertainment studio in Los Angeles. It was exciting. I was able to have meetings in a very famous filmmaker's office, where he played Flight Simulator, one of the applications he was using our expensive equipment for. There was a system in the office, at his house, at a very famous movie star's home in Arizona, and our team was able to participate in this deal. We had a conditional purchase order for a few hundred thousand dollars, but there were no conditions on it.

In the second set of meetings I attended, they asked for more than one million dollars' worth of more equipment and services without actually paying for it. Want to know how the famous studios get so wealthy? They get free equipment, promising to buy more. There was no actual deal. It was a complete misfire. Nope, you can't make this stuff up! Apparently, the Pipeline had been enamored with the well-known studio, the highly visible movie mogul behind it, and had lost sight of the fact they simply wanted to entice the company for no-charge demo equipment, free services, and a carrot for potential future business. In turn, the Pipeline learned that running a company was not like running sales. That's why his stint was short as interim CEO.

Chapter 2 Takeaways

- Functional expertise that you end up developing throughout your career and how you apply it to your path to CEO will have a long-lasting impact on the type of CEO you will become.
- You will already have developed in your functional expertise area how to motivate and inspire people to get the job done successfully. Some of you may have multiple areas of functional expertise and that can be applied as you take on and lead an entire company.
- Hire functional expertise around you. Doing this allows you as a rookie CEO to set direction, as long as you let them do their job. Ask them as many detailed questions as you need to and hold regular leadership team meetings. Don't micromanage them unless there is a serious issue needing your attention.

CHAPTER 3

Track Record, Pedigree, Influences

The final three elements from the rookie's background that shape them for their new CEO role include (1) their track record in whatever functional role they have held, (2) their pedigree, which is their educational background, college, advanced degrees, family wealth, and lifestyles, and (3) whatever their influences are. In this chapter you'll find a snapshot of how these may drive rookie CEO behavior.

Track Record

In sports, there are born competitors and winners. If the rookie is one of these types, they will likely be successful. It's all about the winning attitude. Tom Brady comes to mind. He has been a winner at every level, even when the experts did not believe he was that good. As a sixth round draft choice (the 199th player selected in the 2000 draft) of the New England Patriots, he has had a chip on his shoulder for his entire professional career. He proved he is a winner year in and year out for many years and many divisional and Super Bowl championships. You don't have to like him or his team, but study his competitive behavior and winning attitude for tips on how to lead.

Some leaders never win, they may or may not succeed. In their rookie CEO role, they have to prove themselves once they achieve the position. In their previous roles, did they exit (get acquired or do an IPO)? Did their company grow to be a market leader? Winners know how to create, grow, and scale. Winners can create market opportunities. Winners can build high-powered teams and get the best out of them, making everyone around them better.

Future performance is predicted by past performance and is used by recruiters and boards of directors in hiring the rookie CEO. This is why all CEOs have resumes (CVs) and artists have portfolios.

Pedigree

As mentioned previously, pedigree is not always the major factor in success for the rookie CEO. Some of these rookies have a chip on their shoulder and are scrappy, street smart, and just make things happen. Michael Dell selling PC expansion cards out of his trunk is an example. Nothing would stop him in his early days from selling his product and learning about his customers while providing top-notch customer service.

Highly educated rookies graduate from top business schools, such as Harvard Business School, Northwestern's Kellogg School of Management, Stanford Graduate School of Business, Oxford, and many other top schools. These rookies plan on being CEO and train for it their entire lifetimes. Many do go on to be incredibly successful CEOs, but they are rookies in the beginning. All rookie CEOs make mistakes as they learn, grow, and gain experience. Neither formal education nor an Ivy league education matters to be a successful rookie CEO.

Rookies have successes and failures, but their pedigree criteria drive the rookie CEO's behavior. I can't tell you how many times I have met a rookie CEO whose first statement to me is this: "I graduated from Harvard!" This is to make sure that I know they will be the smartest in the room and that I should never question them. Don't get me wrong, Harvard and other top business school MBAs are smart and good people, but arrogance can come with this pedigree. For the rookie who brings both intelligence and wisdom to the party, where they went to school or grew up has no relevance. Their PPLC does have direct relevance.

Influences

What are the outside influences for the rookie CEO? LinkedIn provides the ability to follow influencers, so you can often find who the influencers are for rookie CEOs if they choose this vehicle to follow their favorites. There are many types of influencers, from successful companies to successful executives. Examples include Sir Richard Branson, Steve Jobs, Bill Gates, Mark Cuban, Peter Drucker, Gary Vaynerchuk, Jeff Weiner, Jack Welch, and many more. Often, the culture the rookie builds will be similar to those created by their influencers.

The Cyclone idolized Carley Fiorina, a former presidential candidate and a CEO herself. I saw them both give keynote speeches at different technology events about a year apart. I closed my eyes, did not have to look at their slides, and the words were nearly identical. Influence to the speech level is not really uncommon when the rookie has a clear influencer. When the Cyclone got to our company, even though we were smaller, the rookie attempted to recreate Carley's larger company culture and structure. Some of these attempts were actually good, but many were too expensive to implement. The Cyclone was a rookie CEO learning what could, and could not, be transferred from a previous influencer's style and approach.

As a rookie CEO, use your influencers to guide you, but be yourself and create your own identity. I guarantee, once you tell family, friends, and business connections you are about to become a CEO, you will be barraged with advice. Some advice may be excellent, you just need to find out what advice falls into this category! This book can provide a baseline to help leverage your outside influences, so you'll head into your new role with a best-laid plan. Your model for success will be a combination of your plan and how you handle unplanned distractions.

Chapter 3 Takeaways

- Typically, the best indicator of future success is past success. Your track record of success will follow you.
- Being a rookie CEO is hard, don't be fooled by your previous senior-level success which gets more challenging when you expand your scope as CEO.
- You don't need to be a graduate of a top business school to be a successful CEO.
- Along your entire career, as you grow, build your list of influencers. They can be people, books, movements, or mentors, but keep track of them all as you will apply things that influence every day of your CEO role, especially in your rookie period.

SECTION 2
PHILOSOPHY

He who thinks great thoughts,
   often makes great errors.

—Martin Heidegger

CHAPTER 4

Foundation to Future

Philosophy, the second P in PPLC, is as critical to the rookie CEO's success as anything along the way. Each new leader owns their philosophy and their foundation of trust through their personal values and ethics; how they value people and ideas; how they live and work; how they build teams; and, in general, how they will manage and lead the company. The transformation of how the rookie integrates their philosophy into their new role will dictate the entire foundation for the company and set the stage for the culture and working environment going forward.

These philosophies are different for every rookie CEO, and typically, for the hiring body too, meaning the board of directors that hires what they want the company to be next, which can be very different from where it has been. Of course, a startup rookie CEO may not have realized their philosophy quite yet. The following chapters deliver a review of some of the philosophies that I experienced from CEOs both at startups and established companies.

The established company rookie CEO brings their former experience and methodologies to their new role. They will have a vision, share this vision, and build the management team from both existing people and new hires, which almost always includes their former colleagues. They are coming from a former vice president or chief role, depending on their backgrounds. Do they value loyalty? Innovation? Delegation? Budget and money management? Confrontation or collaboration? Risk-taking? Do they inspire and motivate people, or are they ruthless, high-energy "drive change" at all costs? As you can see, these all can bring totally new and unique philosophies and change the way a company is led. There are many variables that encompass the rookie CEO's philosophical approach.

Philosophies That Build or Bust Respect

Want to lose the respect of your team? Here is an example of how to accomplish this. Upon arrival at our company, one of the first tasks this rookie CEO gave to me was a CD with documentation on it from the previous company and the following instructions: "Do a 'find/replace all' on the previous company name to our company name, edit it to make sure all references to the old company are changed, and this will become our new process and policy." Wow! I was flabbergasted. I shared this with my closest colleague who would be impacted by this, and we got a telling insight into the kind of boss this rookie CEO would be. That was the beginning. It got worse from there. Was this rookie's standard operating procedure to copy and steal others' processes or technology? Talk about a shady philosophy! It raised many questions about what else we'd need to watch out for and the integrity of the rookie was at risk. Yet again, you can't make this stuff up!

Want to gain the respect of the team? Be a leader with one-on-one meetings, learning about each functional area. After that, brainstorm with your team, gradually introducing the direction you will be leading everyone in. This was done by only one of the rookie CEOs, and it was not only appreciated, but it built relationships and allowed the newly minted CEO to make everyone feel a part of the new direction. Great collaborator skills. Of course, being great at collaboration might mean they are not good at confrontation, which turned out to also be true. This same rookie missed the boat with one of our acquisitions, allowing the acquired company to essentially do what they wanted, which did cause many issues over the next few years.

Rookie CEOs and leaders bring to their new roles a philosophy of how they will build their foundation of respect with the management team and employees. Communication and collaboration make a key component of building this foundation and getting to know the team. At the same time, the rookie's philosophy regarding when projects run into problems is also a key component to successfully leading the company in times of difficulty. These philosophies can build or bust a company and drive the rookie's success (or lack thereof)!

Fitting Their Previous Philosophy into a New Role

One of the former GMs/COOs told me that in the rookie CEO role, keep your general philosophy that worked before in the new role. Be prepared to shape and tweak your philosophy that you bring to the new role, but build on what works.

The Cyclone brought some methods of operation from previous roles where the company was managed through the senior leadership team's weekly meetings. However, after the first couple of meetings, the Cyclone started to pick one executive per week to throw under the bus in front of the team. A strong message was delivered, but it was painful and should have been private between the CEO and VP. One day the wrong VP was thrown under the bus, and it eventually led to the rookie's demise. This attack philosophy was one the rookie felt would drive the team to "rise above," but, in fact, it backfired. One perspective was this rookie was trying to disrupt the management team in preparation of acquiring her former colleagues to replace the disrupted management team. The takeaway here is for executives that report to the rookie, keep your eyes open to these secretive types of moves.

Startup rookie CEO, the Dealmaker, who followed the founder CEO, the Builder, brought a philosophy of spending money to gain customers through his sales background philosophy, "Money motivates." He was on the right path, but the rookie CEO needs to lead the company and make sure all groups have budget monies to get their jobs done and delivered, not just money for the "fun stuff." A couple of examples were the Dealmaker's over-spending on some marketing projects and underspending on getting products to market through development. The founders of this company were engineers, and after we announced the products at a tradeshow, the key developers told us one week later about delays in the delivery. Being from a sales background, the Dealmaker thought money motivated everyone. Here is my favorite story, which is the best example of this misguided concept.

Rookie CEO Story: The Wheelbarrow

This story falls into the category of "you can't make this stuff up!" This would have been one of the biggest blunders in history, if ever executed, but even bringing up the idea to the founders in a small private meeting marked the beginning of the end for the Dealmaker. The Dealmaker's early philosophy of leading and expecting results simply with a cash bonus uncovered a flaw in thinking. It's not just about money for everyone.

The company had spent millions of dollars developing new technology, which we had just launched at two trade shows. The interested customer list was a top-tier list of household names to qualify operation in their labs prior to production deployment. One week after the second big tradeshow launch, where we had won a "best of show" category award, the development team told us we would be delayed for six months or more due to technology issues. This is a killer because once you have momentum and lose it, it is much harder to get it back without a restart.

The idea, as presented by the Dealmaker, was to offer the engineering team $100 thousand in cash, rolled into the meeting in a wheelbarrow, with stacks of bills directly in front of the engineers. Along with this amazing wheelbarrow of cash, we'd tell the engineers, "Deliver on this date, and this cash is yours to split!" If they could not hit that date, "Deliver on this second date, and you will get three-quarters of this cash." The younger engineers would think, "Wow! This is pretty cool!" At least, that's what the Dealmaker assumed the engineers would think.

This proposal had "disaster" written all over it. The Dealmaker disagreed with this "disaster" viewpoint at first. The Dealmaker was from a sales background where money motivates people. As an engineer by background and degree, I shared with him that technical problems and challenges drove engineers, money being further down the list of priorities than it is for salespeople.

When the Dealmaker chose to present the wheelbarrow-of-cash idea to the engineering leaders and founders anyway, it was not well-received. In fact, the opposite. "You don't trust us! You just don't believe us!" they said, for they interpreted this cash offer as the Dealmaker not giving credence to the delay they said they would need. Once trust is gone, it is nearly impossible to gain back. Especially in a startup, regardless of how much cash has been raised.

Let me add too that when the Dealmaker initially raised this idea, we called the local police to see if they would be able to come to the office the day we were to roll the wheelbarrow of cash into the offices. They responded, "Thieves that hear about this will show up with automatic weapons for that much cash, they already show up for a few hundred dollars let alone $100K!" They advised against it. As I already shared, this didn't stop the Dealmaker from suggesting this idea to the engineering leaders and founders.

No, we never did do it, but by simply presenting the idea to the founders, the Dealmaker showed poor judgment, a move that put his job on the line.

The lesson learned is to clearly understand what motivates all the people on your team and in the company, and what the downside might be if an idea is not well-received. Knowing these motivations and incorporating them into your philosophical approach to different people is essential. Also, always consider the top five questions or concerns that may arise before choosing to present and share a radical idea. And if even the police think it's a bad idea, listen to them.

Communication Philosophy: Clarity or Ambiguity

Another major philosophy is around communication with everyone—upwards with the board of directors and downwards with not only the management team but all employees. Does the rookie openly share strategies and report business results at town hall meetings? Does the CEO talk to everyone about highest-level company priorities? Or does the rookie purposefully and strategically communicate in a secretive or ambiguous manner?

The rookie can provide clarity or ambiguity by design. I have worked for both types. Some rookies like ambiguity where others are absolutely focused on clarity. The Opportunist was clearly focused on clarity using SMART goals and individual scorecards on a quarterly basis to eliminate the ambiguity that had been normal operation previously. Previously the management team had not all known their priorities or what to deliver, as was obvious by simply sitting in my first management team meetings, so the Opportunist's clarity was needed. Some CEOs implement MBOs, management by objectives; OKRs, objectives and key results; or KPIs, key performance indicators for setting goals, which are often used for raises and bonuses. It's all in the philosophy of the rookie CEO and their management team, or not. We discuss metrics several more times in upcoming chapters.

Secretive Operating Philosophy: the communication philosophy of the rookie CEO has significant impact on employees and the management team. When the rookie's philosophical model is more on the secretive side than the open side, it can cause discomfort among people. When employees or managers don't know for sure, they make stuff up. Try it sometime by testing this with your team. Make it something that does not hurt the company.

Three rookies fell into this philosophical model where they chose not to or could not share key happenings with the senior leadership team jointly, but selectively told different team members different parts of the story. It's hard to determine if it was due to ego, arrogance, an agreement with the board of directors, or just distrust that drove them to act this way. It was frustrating to those who did not get the details. Later, in a team meeting, the rookie would say, "You all know about this, I told you!" But then a handful of the team would respond that they didn't know. This caused back-channel discussions about the rookie CEO and their leadership philosophy, and it did not motivate executives to perform at the top of their game.

I have been on both sides of this example, knowing it was done this way. What was disappointing about this secretive behavior was that others could have helped if the topics had been openly discussed, or if the rookie had met with everyone, they could have received some coaching and different perspectives before making their decision. These situations are likely to occur at many companies. It is also true that on many occasions, the CEO simply cannot tell the entire team everything happening at the board-of-director level. This is hard for the team to understand, but it is more standard operation than not.

Closed Door Leadership: while closed door leadership may be true of all CEOs and many executives to varying extents, it is the source of starting rumors and showing employees you are secretive in your leadership style. When the CEO, especially a rookie CEO, stays in their office with the door closed, it promotes a lack of communication. Three of my featured rookies suffered from this type of behavior. Even if they knew it, they chose to ignore feedback and always had a reason: "I was on a call with the board," "I was working on salary and payroll items," or it could be simply they wanted peace and quiet. Regardless of why, it leaves a bad taste in the mouth of the employees. It can go against the very culture that the company publicly espouses, such as open communication, transparency, and collaboration. This behavior tends to lead to rumors, as people will make up a story about what is being discussed in the closed door meeting. To be clear, I am not suggesting that the rookie CEO never closes their door, at times it is required, but do not make it a daily habit where your people start counting and logging the number of hours or times you do this.

Communication and BCC: have you ever used "BCC," which stands for "blind carbon copy," on your emails? Don't, even if you are ever tempted. There are rookies who have BCC-ed, meaning they included secret additional recipients on emails. At least in one case, the rookie was caught as the BCC-ed recipient "replied all." Word travels fast with this type of mistake. BCC is used to hide recipients of the email from seeing anyone who is BCC-ed. Using BCC is generally acknowledged as deceitful. One potential danger is if a BCC-ed recipient does a "reply all" (as was the case I just told you about), it will identify to all the email's recipients (meaning, those who were not aware that this other person also received the email) the action was done. This is a philosophy that will truly hurt any thoughts about your integrity. There are a couple of use cases where BCC is effective: (1) BCC-ing yourself and (2) sending general newsletters to people who do not know each other and you want to protect their email addresses.

Cost-Controlling Philosophy

Another philosophy that has consequences if not executed perfectly is driven by the fact that costs must be controlled regardless of company stage or size. In businesses that have limited budgets and resources, a "zero sum resource game" might be to try and execute something differently but with no change in budget, resources, or people. In my 30-plus years at the senior level in many companies, I have been on or led many "tiger teams" assembled from matrixed organizations to attack a short-term problem. These problems may have been in building pipeline, closing a deal, bringing a project back on track, righting a sagging brand, or continuous improvement types of teams.

The key story here was that twice, one rookie created a tiger sales team while on an airplane because the board of directors was breathing down his throat. He did not collaborate with the team; he just executed it. At the time, as a small company we could not hire anyone else, we could not increase spend; thus, we had to make a team of existing people. In this case it was the same sales personnel in the company who were joined by several non-sales folks, which the rookie felt could work. We already had a sales process, a CRM, and marketing automation, but the rookie wanted a new process that he could take control over his way, which was using Excel to track what was already in the existing database driven by a sales and marketing automation tool. Those on the "tiger team" who built the existing process were generally unhappy, not listened to, but were on point to "train" the new folks and work within the new unproven process. There may be different takeaways from this example, but to me there were two: (1) this was a #bigfail because time was wasted from the tiger team's normal jobs, and (2) this rookie's philosophy that any-one can sell to sophisticated prospects and be a sales participant was flawed. Talk to the sales team, get buy-in on an approach and how they may have seen this work in the past, and then apply it to your purposeful goal of the tiger team. Credit to the rookie for trying something new, but it just did not work.

The "zero sum resource game" is a philosophy for getting critical short-term projects done without any additional budget spend. There were times in my past when the zero sum resource game via tiger team has worked, but it was usually in a much larger company that had a short-term, high-priority project that could be done and absorbed more easily. In hindsight, if the rookie in the above example had sat down with the management and sales teams, we jointly might have had a tiger team format that may have been more successful if every-one bought in and participated in the strategy and execution plan, but in reality, if you make no changes and do the same things, it usually leads to no change in results.

Loyalty Philosophy

As mentioned previously, hiring friends is not unusual, but it has its advantages and caveats. Hiring trusted people is excellent. What happens if it does not work? Here is a story.

This is very common for rookie CEOs. If they had a loyal team previously, they will want to bring them into their new company. Most often, these loyal folks get promotions, ready or not, and the rookie gets a loyal team with built-in trust. Inheriting a team is more challenging for rookies. I have been on both sides of the equation, so I see this model clearly. The challenge is what happens when hiring previous teams and friends does not work out. It can and does happen, but many rookies do not take actions due to their loyalty. I have talked to rookies who have admitted to me they wished they took action earlier than later. So be careful as a rookie CEO hiring friends. It does not always bring what you want, and you can't always protect them, even if you want to. Do not let this idea stop you from hiring friends because they can help and they are trusted. Just lead the team and be open and honest with them along the way. Communication with friends is different than communication with others.

Let me give two examples of complete loyalty of a friend that was hired by the rookie CEO. Typically, the roles the friends get are good and well-paying in exchange for their loyalty. The first example was when rookie CEO's employee friend A fell out of favor with another of the rookie CEO's new hire friend B, even though employee A was a solid resource, employee A was let go regardless of 100% loyalty. This may damage any friendship between the rookie and employee A. The second example was when investors changed their mind about the importance of a function that the rookie CEO had hired a friend to lead. Even though it had been successful and the friend was doing great work, the rookie was told to eliminate the position. In both cases, the rookie CEO hired a friend 100% loyal to them, but other influences forced the rookie to eliminate the friend, even though it was not deserved. It just goes with the territory and can damage long-term friendships. Over time, the eliminated friend gets over it, but it is difficult when loyalty is one way.

Remember, as CEO—rookie or not—the board of directors is your boss and investors are the bankers.

Philosophy on Open Conference Calls

This philosophy falls both under loyalty and under clear or ambiguous communication. This philosophy has been around since speaker phones appeared in conference rooms and built into phones. Once the speaker is on, it's like open mic night at karaoke! But conference calls can be filled with peril. No one knows who is on an open call. This story is about a new rookie call before the new job started, and I point out a couple of my meeting mantras, which might help some readers (and which we'll look at again in the final chapter).

One rookie started with their loyalties to their former employees before actually starting the new job. This rookie held conference calls with the new management team and called from their current conference room location. The rookie's current staff was on the call without our (i.e., the new management team's) knowledge. The rookie was planning on bringing these folks to our company eventually but never announced them on the call. We learned this later. You never know who is on an audio conference call.

Heads up on all conference calls: if you start talking about someone who you think is not on the call, but they are silently listening, this can put you in peril. Many CEOs (and other executives) play this game. It is devious, and if the CEO does utilize this type of approach, it tells a lot about their integrity and philosophy.

This situation uncovers two of my mantras for meetings: (1) never answer a question that is not asked and (2) never answer a question that is meant for someone else already in the room. I have seen these two mantras violated dozens of times in my career. In reality, it's a life mantra for anything from family to interviewing. All you can do is be wrong or disrupt a train of thought of the CEO's (or other person's) intentions.

Philosophy on Signature Authority

This is in my philosophy section because it actually happened to really hurt the rookie. Hint to ALL CEOs, new or not, is to never give up final top-level signature authority. You can delegate it to someone you trust, but do not give blanket authority to finance or anyone for all expenses as final sign-off. In startups, usually the CEO signs for everything, perhaps with a trusted second executive if the CEO is not available. As a VP, I have been the delegated to, trusted signature on multiple occasions.

I have a few stories in this category but only one that had a serious effect on the company's fate. Signature authority is sacred. If you are a startup rookie CEO whose weakness is financial, you are likely to hire a financial executive at the senior level. I have been the second in command on multiple occasions and always followed protocol. Typical senior-level finance executives understand the movement of cash and securities, and are to be clearly never left with the highest level and final signature authority over and above the CEO—the CEO must always maintain this function. In larger companies this may not be necessary in all cases, but in smaller startups and mid-sized companies, cash is king and bank account management is a critical factor for success.

One rookie I worked for gave top-tier signature authority to the vice president of finance, which turned out to be part of the company's most critical decision points in its history. The finance executive ended up misguiding quite a bit of money, and no one could catch him until long after the rookie CEO had left the company. The finance executive was "stealing" by misappropriating cash from the company to his own personal accounts. I was able to help the team that succeeded the rookie CEO because I knew one of the folks involved in the next stage of the company, and we learned about the misuse of that very thing—signature authority—in the missteps the finance executive made. Because you, as the rookie CEO, are accountable for cash and costs across the entire company, make this a part of your philosophy.

Philosophy Regarding Meetings

Meetings are part of the day-to-day operation of every company. The rookie's philosophy on meetings will be implemented; thus, it is important to have an idea about what might and might not work as a rookie CEO. Here are some stories from my featured rookies.

Most companies I worked for had offsite meetings, so why are they addressed here as "a story"? For starters, if you are the rookie CEO, and you keep talking about an offsite meeting to help focus the team and strategy and project priorities, then have the meeting. One rookie just talked, and all it did was upset the management team and never resolved the open issues. In fact, this particular rookie was one of the secretive ones and resolved the issues one by one with only "need-to-know" individuals. Since there had been many discussions, however, the team that did not participate ended up being left out.

Now for some of the most intriguing offsite meetings worth sharing: Silicon Valley will be my first example. The venture capital dollars are significant, and parties and offsite events are second to none! From renting out museums for private events to hiring stretch limo services for all employees roundtrip to ensure no drunk driving, no stone was left unturned. From golf in Half Moon Bay, to a dinner in the hills, we had offsite meetings for the management team, board of director meetings, portfolio events sponsored by the venture capital company with guest speakers, such as Steve Blank and Steve Young. These events are lifelong memories and learning events.

There were two other companies that had golf outings for management team meetings or board of director meetings. One other was a venture capital sponsored board meeting at a private golf club in Cape Cod, and the other was at a Pacific Ocean golf club where all 18 greens were overlooking the ocean. The latter was for management meetings and partner meetings when deals were being made in golf carts! "It's the art of the deal" was a phrase I heard a few times when planning these events and meetings. I have to admit they all were fantastic and great motivational events!

Another "offsite" meeting example that leaves memories are "at the rookie's home," and the management team was invited. There were three of these types of events. One was an all-employee event for Halloween and required costumes. This rookie lived in a multi-million-dollar home and left many employees with the impression that the event was "all about him," not the employees. I think the idea was excellent, but make it about the people! There was no business except for side discussions at this event.

The second example was another all-employee all-day event on a weekend at a nice million-dollar home with lots of acreage. Parties all day and night, there were no issues with the younger employees at this event as all were happy, had fun, and many stayed overnight somewhere on the property. It was a one-time event that was memorable. It was all about the people. Games for all age groups and physical capabilities.

The final offsite at the rookie CEO's private home was a true business meeting. Everyone had to fly to the rookie's location, which was not at the corporate location. It was quite the event. This rookie was a bit more modest than the two previously discussed, but it was wealth none the same. This rookie broke the team into working groups within the house, then the teams came back to present their group results. On one occasion, this rookie brought at least one employee into the bedroom for private discussions that later brought rumors to the company. Hard to forget these types of events. Personally, I love these types of events because they are so memorable and can help management teams gain focus and build camaraderie.

Chapter 4 Takeaways

- Your philosophy is shaped from your early years through your entire life as you mature and grow through experiences.
- In my opinion, you can't train for modifying your philosophy. Experiences can influence philosophy over time, as you learn, and you can gain breadth of philosophy every day, every

month, and every year of your career. Your time as a rookie CEO will be built on your philosophy. Keep what works in your new role.

- As you prepare for your future CEO role, organize your thoughts and structure how you will lead, motivate, inspire, manage, hire, delegate, recruit, and every other element as described in this chapter. Remember, this is the first time you will own all functional departments, and it is exponentially harder than owning a single function.

SECTION 3
LEADERSHIP STYLE

Before you are a leader, success is all about growing yourself. When you become a leader, success is all about growing others.

—Jack Welch

CHAPTER 5

Elements

L eadership styles are built on many different elements. To start, management style itself is an element of leadership, and most rookies move up from a functional leadership role, which managed a business function and people. Their individual management style was developed previously, and now that they are a CEO, it is time for them to grow from day-to-day functional-management type of leadership into CEO leadership.

Human Attributes and Success

There are human attributes that the rookie will bring to the company in their new role. These are critical success factors. How does the rookie treat people? Do they come with a purpose and a focus to succeed? Are they competitive and aggressive? Think about this and the rookie: if they bring a technical background, they may be innovative. If they are more visionary and business-oriented (i.e., "Let's change the world"), they are trendsetters, visionary, and more big-picture type of leaders. Some rookies are combinations of these, where they may be technical but also have a terrific vision and love to be trendsetters. They don't need market data and analysis because they are so innovative that the market does not yet know what it needs, but the rookie with a vision and purpose who is innovative moves ahead as fast as possible.

Leaders who bring initiative and are on a mission, are likely to know market trends, are great at anticipating market needs and taking calculated risks, and can be top-notch rookie CEOs and leaders. Rookie CEOs that translate their perspectives into initiatives can inspire the team and engage the employees to move their mission forward. They bring an intellect to the rookie CEO position and a confidence in leading the company. They build a high-performance leadership team and coach them, not micromanage them, and establish a solid foundation for success. This foundation by nature will motivate the team and empower managers to execute and achieve results while setting the company up for future growth.

Rookie CEOs at established companies will inherit a leadership team. Most often, the rookie will vet the team and decide who stays and who goes. They will choose to end up with a team of A players (extraordinary leaders) and B players (solid citizens) in some combination. The team makeup depends on the rookie's coaching skills and if they are hands-off or hands-on. In my case, two examples are the General who was a good coach and hands-off, and the Dealmaker who was a people person and hands-on.

Leading and Letting Go

Rookie CEOs that can be engaging are great listeners, ask a lot of questions, and work closely with the high-performance management team. Once decisions are made, the rookie simply lets the team execute and makes sure goals are set, project status meetings are on track, and priorities are clear. For rookies, it may be difficult to let go, but it is part of a success formula. The rookie needs to build in checkpoints once they let go, so they are satisfied with progress and create and manage a process to ensure everything stays on track.

In the new world of work-from-home, will the rookie demand all employees work in the office, or do they support and enable remote workers? Trends are moving towards a large portion of the workforce working remotely if they can, thus saving costs on building space and utilities. These types of things clearly have an impact on the company's future success, budgets, and culture. New collaboration tools are available and are better than ever since more CEOs allow more remote workers. What will happen in the future? What will work for the rookie's new company?

Many leaders provide thought leadership and get invited to be keynote speakers. If the rookie is a visionary and is changing the world, they will be invited to conferences as a keynote speaker. Other executives and managers may be invited to be panelists and speakers, but the CEOs get the keynotes. These are excellent vehicles to get the company message out to market.

As a new leader, will the rookie bring focus and SMART goals, OKRs, or KPIs to the management team? How do they run meetings and assign projects, priorities, and tasks? Are they collaborative, or does the rookie demand and tell everyone what to do? My advice to the rookie is to be collaborative but know where you want to land and drive the discussions to that end point. The Innovatist and the General were quite good at executing that style.

Metrics and Accountability

Another style of leadership is how company metrics are managed and shared. Does the rookie believe in dashboards that are shared amongst all employees or are secretive only for a couple of executives and the rookie? There are many metrics to track from sales, pipeline, inventory, cash flows, expenses, returns, and on and on. I have observed that rookies who share a well-designed and ever-evolving dashboard with all employees, even if it is "sanitized" for sharing with employees, are very well-received by most employees.

One area that I have seen rookie CEOs fall short, is being and holding others accountable to both the board of directors and the employees. This is a style the rookie brings to their new role. Senior leadership has no problems with accountability, as long as the measured goals are achievable, measurable, and align with corporate direction.

Several of the featured rookies displayed tendencies to be controlling micromanagers, at least at times. As a new CEO, you have to let go and lead, not manage. It is very hard to do this for most rookie CEOs. The best I worked for were great at delegation, held their teams accountable, and the CEO was accountable to the board of directors. Controlling every aspect of every project is "balloon busting" to the management team. In fact, if the CEO attends low-level meetings and makes decisions that clearly are outside the CEO realm, it has a negative impact on productivity and employee satisfaction.

Planning: Focused or Fickle

Planning is a critical success factor to build the company strategy that the rookie will lead and the executives and managers will implement. There are proven methods of planning, sometimes using outside consultants but also utilizing key team members. There are also poor methods of planning. Few, if any, executives will respect or enjoy a "seat-of-the-pants" type of rookie CEO because priorities are never clear, things change, and it feels like there is no plan.

Seat-of-the-pants type of planning runs rampant across many smaller companies, but for rookie CEOs, this can be a damaging and disruptive method of operation. Having no real plan potentially causes a misunderstanding of priorities, deliverables, and milestones, and can ruin a culture. I have no doubt there have been lucky companies with the right funding, the right products, and a couple of breaks that succeeded without a plan of some type. A plan can even be a whiteboard or flipchart developed plan, but having a plan is an important factor to succeed.

If the rookie constantly changes the plan, employees get confused about priorities or projects, can get stressed, and it truly disrupts the momentum of a strong team. You may never get to the targeted goals.

Some of our featured rookie CEOs used PowerPoint slides but changed them weekly based on discussions with customers, the board of directors, an outside contact, or even another employee.

The antithesis of this is "analysis paralysis" where the rookie does a detailed plan and continues to analyze the numbers, the projects, and priorities, and changes sometimes multiple times per day. Both ends of this spectrum cause issues among the investors, board of directors, and employees. One caveat here is that lead customers might be driving the changes, and for this one scenario, the rookie CEO needs to have a team on board to help manage the demands from the customer and communication with employees.

Three of the nine featured rookie CEOs would read a book or online article or talk to a CEO peer group, and the next day our plan would change. This defeats SMART goals, creates ambiguity, and really upsets all levels of managers and key team members. It is hard to gain momentum and move forward with this type of operational philosophy.

Now, I am not saying that the rookie should not do these things. In fact, the rookie should talk with customers, partners, trusted management team members, or others, and weigh modifications for the business, but they should not change plans daily and for no reason. Change for customers, market dynamics, and making the solution better through refinement is good, but the rookie needs to do this in an organized and clear manner.

Rookie CEO Story: The Too Tall Order

One example of this seat-of-the-pants style of planning, is when a customer told our rookie CEO if we hit this unrealistic date, they would potentially deploy in an application, and that caused significant disruption within the company. Engineers said it would not be possible, operations said it would be difficult, if not impossible to deliver, but the rookie was not going to be denied. The product was really a prototype, and the first time the product would be deployed in a live environment. Daily and weekly all-employee meetings were held by the rookie to ask if not beg people to work harder, longer hours, to make this opportunity happen. This was unplanned and out of the ordinary, but the rookie would not admit it would not work until we tried to deliver a non-working product even though people did work long hours, harder, and some people did get sick. I get it that the rookie really wanted this project and it would have been incredible, but it was an abnormally tall order that was not achievable. Engineers' schedules were disrupted, weekends were lost, as well as holidays, and some people took time to recover from this situation. A few folks looked for new jobs shortly after this fire drill, but no one left.

If you are the rookie CEO and have a similar opportunity, to be an outstanding leader in a situation like the one given, take your top three executives and maybe top two or three engineers and operations folks, and build a plan together and see what is needed that you may not have to hope to achieve the goals. By getting buy-in from the team, with their ideas, you may have a fighting chance to deliver.

Chapter 5 Takeaways

- Your leadership style will have been shaped by your professional career as you progress. Yes, you will own all functional areas in the rookie CEO role, but your leadership style will grow based on your fundamentals.
- Set goals, build a solid team around you, and let them do their jobs in support of your direction, leadership, and goals that you and your team have set together.
- There is never only one way to do anything. Find your way, applying your PPLC, and execute!

CHAPTER 6

Inspiration, Motivation, and Thought Leadership

Each rookie brings to the new role their personal and fundamental approach to people and process. As discussed previously, are they "people first"-oriented or "process first"-oriented? My favorite example is Coach Bill Belichick of the New England Patriots National Football League franchise. The coach is well-known to be "process and system"-oriented and people who choose not to "buy in" or adopt his methods don't stay with the Patriots. The coach is process and system first, and leads with authority. A rookie CEO could follow the Belichick model, and in most organizations people may leave rather quickly if they choose not to buy into the rookie's system. You may not like this coach or team, but you can't argue their team ways and records are winning ones.

My perspective is that people like to be treated with dignity, to be collaborated with by the new rookie, and to be heard, so they will buy into the new CEO's operation. This is where inspiration and motivation come into play. The rookie that displays innovative ways to motivate the team using an inspirational style will earn respect, and the people will align and buy in. They just want to be heard and respected!

Trust As Inspiration

How do you inspire and what can you do as a rookie CEO? Number one is to avoid micromanaging everyone and everything. Set direction and lead. No executive I know appreciates the micromanagement approach, it is the opposite of inspirational! Encourage people to work together by setting goals with clarity—SMART goals can work, but only one of the rookies used SMART goals. As mentioned earlier, some rookies use MBOs, OKRs, or KPIs to set goals and measure performance.

Create an environment where meetings are designed to be agile, short, and progressive, and work on creating or modifying the culture to encourage colleagues to help each other, support each other, and be customer-focused! Communication styles are at the core of inspiration and motivation. Recognize people for trying things and possibly even publicly acknowledge fast failure experimentation and new things to improve, anything from quality to customer success.

Metrics and Motivation

The Opportunist used SMART goals and executed via scorecards, which were assigned to each manager and senior employee. These are essentially performance metrics that drive business success. What are SMART goals? Here's a very brief overview. A SMART goal is one that is:

- S = Specific
- M = Measurable
- A = Actionable

- R = Results-Oriented
- T = Timed

Scorecards turn out to be a terrific vehicle to deliver SMART goals, but they are just one way to execute. Scorecards are simple written objectives clearly delineating deliverables for each executive or manager. In fact, simple whiteboarded target goals can work well too, as can goals listed on a central WIKI or any method that records the goals and expectations of each functional head and manager. If they are open and published on a WIKI or on an intranet somewhere, everyone knows how to help their colleagues and peers.

My experience is that setting specific time-based goals provides the most likely execution success model. However, each of the nine rookies was different. One rookie felt that if you give people goals and they achieve them, they will want bonuses and raises. This situation was not comfortable for those employees used to being recognized for success. There was loyalty towards the company vision to be success-ful, which is what helped this rookie deliver products. In this case, regardless of leadership style, you can keep the team focused to deliver.

CEO Presence and Motivation

Motivation is connected to many facets of the rookie CEO. Philosophy, leadership style, and culture are all impacted by how the rookie moti-vates the team and individuals on the team. Motivation comes in all sizes. From walking around the office, stopping to talk to people, ask-ing how they are doing and how their project is going and how their family is doing, to calling work-from-home team members for the same discussion, in these ways the rookie can keep people motivated by showing interest in them. Most of our featured rookies did talk to people and wander around some, but not all of them did. The Opportunist and the Cyclone stayed office-bound mostly and had people come to them for many meetings except for the senior leader-ship team meetings usually in a boardroom. Employees take notice.

Rookie CEO Story: Kiss-a-Pig Motivation

When I was with the Flyboy's company, we supported many local charities, and we held a "Make-a-Wish" contest in order to raise money for the local foundation. These types of events are both inspiring and motivating, and there are many employees taking part. For this event, each executive in the company got a plastic piggy bank, and employees dropped money into the banks. On the "Make-a-Wish" day when we were to have the charity in-house to present them our donation, we counted the piggy bank cash. The Flyboy won, and the result was he had to kiss a live pig in front of everyone. I have always felt that our team "stuffed" the rookie's piggy bank to make sure he kissed the pig! In reality, this event was fulfilling by helping a "Make-a-Wish" dream come true and by motivating employees. Plus, it made for another zesty "you can't make this stuff up" moment!

Recognition and Gratitude As Motivation

Another excellent form of motivation is to simply say, "Thank you, good job," to people who go the extra mile to create and deliver beyond their normal assignment. Want to learn how to do that? Read and learn from *The One Minute Manager* by Ken Blanchard and Spencer Johnson. This classic is well worth the read if you have not read it yet. This helps in employee praise, or negative feedback or clarification of goals, and it will likely be well appreciated by employees. Communication with clarity is paramount.

Keynotes and Thought Leadership

Many CEOs love doing thought leadership keynotes, authoring papers or books if so inclined, being the spokesperson for the company, and being quoted in press releases. In larger companies, usually the CEO is not the spokesperson, but in startups and smaller companies, this is the case. Being a visionary and changing the world, most conference chairs want you to speak at their event, especially if you are changing the world. Do not be the CEO who does a product announcement in a keynote that is meaningless. The audience will say, "So what?" But if the keynote is about a product or service that changes the game, everyone will want to hear what you have to say! Three of our rookies did keynotes: the General, the Innovatist, and the Flyboy. They were all excellent, engaging speakers in front of larger conference crowds.

Writing and Thought Leadership

Thought leaders should also write blog posts, do byline articles in the media, and always be available to talk to the press and analysts because these key folks want to hear what you have to say!

Today, online platforms including Medium, LinkedIn, Twitter, Facebook, and Instagram provide social vehicles for rookie CEOs to share their thoughts and visions. Some rookies have already built a following from blogging or writing articles, speaking at industry events, podcasts, and public relations activities. These can set the stage for ongoing thought leadership by the rookie CEO.

Chapter 6 Takeaways

- What is your fundamental style of leading—"people first" or "process first"? Pick your method, and build your leadership team around your style, which will enable you to motivate, inspire, and lead around your goals and style.
- Select your tracking method of achieving your goals. Once you are ready, use it from that day on.
- Be the leader. Learn and understand the business, and be a thought leader.
- High energy is contagious, be energetic and enthusiastic.

CHAPTER 7

Focus and Accountability

Many rookie CEOs try to take on and accomplish too much. It happens in many cases. Especially if the rookie was successful in their previous role where they were able to achieve a myriad of tasks and projects. In the new role, the rookie needs to understand and prioritize what will set the bar and what will move the company forward. Some boards of directors are savvy enough to provide this guidance to the rookie to focus, but some boards will also let the rookie go to see where the limitations are. Usually the board will give the rookie three to six months to get into a rhythm, and if they start to flounder, they will provide some unwanted guidance.

I have presented at many board meetings over the past two decades, and I have watched and worked closely with rookies to strategize, present, and deliver, oftentimes helping with the presentation deck. Rookies develop a thick skin or don't make it. They have to be prepared and on point, and are accountable to the board. I have heard multiple times from the board, "You are trying to do too much," to several of these rookies.

When rookies take on too many projects, they have a tendency to disrupt core projects and developments, and I have seen this a few times. A rookie may have had one direction, but projects and priorities changed and led to some of the senior leadership team to whine a lot and be demotivated. There was one rookie who filtered everything bidirectionally with the board. I attended a few board meetings, as did some of my peers, but the truth is he selectively filtered everything both ways. I would not recommend this approach, as it can leave you alone at the top. I am not saying it will not work, but it is not an ideal approach.

Focus and Senior Leadership

Focus can be managed by the rookie CEO using the weekly senior leadership team meeting. You can call it a staff meeting if you wish, but it is a terrific way to basically run the business. Key actions can be assigned, and everyone knows what they are. Priorities can be set jointly, and everyone knows what they are. Decisions can be made if the facts are presented with risks and alternate plans, owners of the projects can be identified, and there should be a scribe who publishes the minutes. Most rookies do have senior leadership staff meetings.

The Cyclone's leadership team was good except, as already mentioned, when this rookie threw vice presidents under the bus—at least one per week. I am a supporter of the 30-, 60-, and 90-day plans that the Cyclone instituted, but not a proponent of the embarrassment of vice presidents each week. If all executives understand the finances, status of sales opportunities, loss or gain of revenues based on budget spend, and delivery of new products, manufactured products, or services, then it becomes a team success or failure, and any issues can be detected early and addressed before they are unrecoverable. In turn, there would never even be the idea of a possibility for throwing any single person under the bus, which also destroys morale, trust, and enthusiasm.

Accountability, Focus, and Forward-Thinking

Forward-thinking is also a core style that influences company direction. Do projects line up with the overall strategy the rookie brought to the new role? Are their solutions "me too" or differentiated and innovative? Think about what hockey player Wayne Gretsky used to say, "Skate to where the puck is going, not to where it has been!" Startups are typically always ahead, but traditional companies are sometimes lost in older delayed projects and have to consider cutting the losses and moving forward. That's why there is a rookie CEO opportunity in the company in the first place!

This is where accountability comes into the day-to-day operation of the company. The most respected leader is the rookie CEO who is accountable to the board. By applying sound general business principles for process, measurable goals, and focus, the rookie will have the key elements needed to move forward and satisfy the board. The rookie will have identified projects that are behind and potentially impacting revenues, but they always can offer a get-well plan based on the team working together. When these don't work well, when any cog in the wheel is not accountable for their assigned goals, and when there's blaming of others on the team, the rookie can gain control by collaborating and discussing alternative ways to achieve goals. Or the rookie can micromanage, fire, or demote someone who misses goals or overcomplicates things for the team, and then everyone suffers. In fact, the rookie's job is at stake if it looks to the board of directors as if the rookie CEO has lost control. Some boards may lose confidence in the rookie, talk to the management team, and learn what the problems are and then take action.

What might be some out-of-control issues? Consider loss of control of the budget, delayed delivery of key projects that have revenues tied to them, a broken process, or a number of related items that cause the management team and the board to lose confidence in the CEO. It happened twice to our featured rookie CEOs. When things get out of control, the rookie operates by "the seat of their pants" or what I call "ready-fire-aim" because they are now under the gun.

The board has already shared the issues with the rookie typically in a straightforward way, and now the rookie is reacting and it usually does not end well.

The only way for the rookie CEO to survive, is to be accountable to the board of directors—their boss—as they can have a heavy influence and can remove the rookie if they choose.

Lousy Focus and Accountability: The Takeover

This happens in several companies of all sizes and stages, but is more common in startups. Let's say one of the key team members does all the heavy lifting on a key project, maybe a key account in a sales situation. Up until the opportunity or project heats up, the rookie literally pays little attention to it, in fact, maybe even discounts it during status meetings. But, once it heats up, the rookie then wants control to drive it their way, and in some cases, the person who did the heavy lifting gets pushed aside. I have seen this and, in fact, have been "that guy" who did the heavy lifting and was moved aside.

If it was only once or twice, I would suggest the employee did not "sell" the project or account, but in the cases I have witnessed or been part of, it was one simple thing: the rookie CEO did not listen to the person who was driving the project or account. The suggestion here is for the rookie to listen. It's okay to have your opinion, but when someone is so passionate about a project or account, challenge the person but listen and help facilitate success, especially if it's aligned with your own strategy! Listen to your team, process the information, and at least be engaged because the employee is working hard to make it happen. Work with the passionate employee.

Chapter 7 Takeaways

- Don't try and do too much, focus—focus—focus.
- Listen to your team members, you'll need a thick skin.

- Be open, as much as you can, with your leadership team—do not filter everything to/from your team.
- Prioritize and be accountable for your deliverables to customers, the board of directors, and your employees, and hold your senior leadership team accountable.

CHAPTER 8

Strategy

Every rookie CEO will own their strategy. If the rookie joins a company with a strategy, they will review and modify it as they see fit. Each company will be different, in a different stage, have different bank accounts and different people. Being a rookie, it's all new, even if they had a similar experience as an executive previously.

CEOs own the strategy and direction of the company. If the investors or board of directors think they own it, you have the recipe for failure. The CEO owns strategy and direction. Strategies in all companies are critical success factors. To execute, the rookie needs to align the senior leadership team, who, in turn, aligns their employees. Strategies can go bust or be successful. What does it take to have a successful and executable strategy?

A well-rounded and complete business plan from the highest level considers market conditions and the environmental situation around the strategy or plan. If a written plan is the tool, use it. Update it. Discuss it. Prioritize it. Manage it. Develop SMART goals. Tracking the market conditions—including competitive situations and environmental situations from the financial market health and dynamics—will help the rookie lead the change required.

It's the leadership team and the rookie CEO's responsibility to execute with their eyes open to drive the plan. What needs to be considered? Understanding customer needs, budget availability, competitive needs, social trends, global macro-level events, competitive moves, and misconceptions in any of these areas. On the inside of the company, are the goals achievable and realistic? Is the plan too complex and can it be simplified? Does the team buy into the execution and achievability of the plans?

I have seen failure when goals are unrealistic from day one and the team has said so; and I have seen success by simplifying the project, aligning the goals with the team, executing, and gaining complete buy-in. Rookie CEOs who show tactics of "I can make this happen" without proof points and only by creating fear and demand around hitting unrealistic dates will fail.

Rookie CEO Story: Offshore Brilliance

One rookie strategy that was successful if not brilliant was the offshore development for user interface and application software. It was challenging to hire affordable engineers in the corporate location, so the rookie secured a contract with an offshore team. It was far less expensive, and the major key to success was to manage and integrate the offshore team into the core development and test team. Daily meetings across the globe were held to keep the offshore team on target and focused. Another benefit of offshore development is that there are no office distractions on a daily basis. There is a team lead in the offshore location and team leads of the corporate development and test teams. As long as the project management tools are universal, the project is well-documented, and communication is daily and open, this can work well.

This same rookie had challenges manufacturing the hardware side of the business, so again went offshore, not just for components, but for subsystems that get assembled into the final system. While executing that, the rookie also drove this as a second source manufacturing location, which took some time but eventually was proven to be successful in both saving time and money, and achieving readiness to scale. For both software and hardware, one major element of success is to bring clarity of direction, timelines, milestones, and specifications. Offshore always requires particularly good communication and clarity. Of course, this is always true everywhere, including the home office, but is especially true offshore.

Chapter 8 Takeaways

- CEOs own the strategy.
- Align mission, vision, and the plan, and then execute the strategy.
- Involve the leadership team.
- Think creatively when solving difficult and challenging issues.

SECTION 4
CULTURE

In determining the right people,
the good-to-great companies placed greater
weight on character attributes than on specific
educational background, practical skills,
specialized knowledge, or work experience.

—Jim Collins
Business consultant
and author of *Good to Great*

CHAPTER 9

Culture

Holder to Riley
culture change
wanted

The C part of PPLC is culture. Culture is something that emerges under the rookie CEO. Culture can change with a new CEO, rookie or not. Sometimes the change is by design. Other times the existing culture is not the ideal one, and when the board hires the new CEO, they may want this change. The board may also choose to maintain the culture. It all depends on the situation.

Can a new rookie CEO totally change the culture? You bet they can. The General brought in his own sales VP on day one, as he was coming over from a large public company. The General had a plan. Over the next two to three years, he brought in 26 people from his old company at manager, director, and vice president levels. His philosophy was that his trust levels in previous loyal team members was paramount to anyone who was at the new company when he took over as CEO. This turned the culture into a mini-version of his previous company, and he was happy with that result. We'll visit this story again at the end of this chapter.

Culture Code As Roadmap

Many companies build and stand by their culture codes, which provide a roadmap for how the company acts, how employees act, and how they operate and make decisions. I have led or helped create culture codes in multiple companies. You can find companies that publish their culture codes such as Zappos, HubSpot, and Microsoft, which are good examples. You can find their culture codes on the company websites. Employees embrace the culture code, live by it, and hire by it. Many will swear by the culture code to build world-class environments and high-performance companies.

An example of a culture code might include core competencies such as trust, inspiration, respect, collaboration, optimism, passion, commitment, humanity, a caring disposition, engagement, and team-orientation. In some companies they create a cross-functional team of people, including human resources, to work together for a few days, weeks, or over a period of time to actually build and document the culture code. Many companies post the code in every meeting or conference room, and print it on the back of business cards and many other locations to continuously remind people of it. This type of process can be adapted to work in every size company.

A couple of other things that may become part of the culture include sports leagues such as softball, tennis, golf, happy hours, dress codes, open communications, open offices, employee recognition, reviews and raises, and even layoffs. Nothing is off limits, but the leadership team and rookie CEO should be accountable to create and lead a culture code that moves the company forward, makes the company a great place to work, and makes employees thrilled and productive to work there. Great cultures attract great people.

Creating a Code

In my career, not all rookie CEOs bought into the culture code. In fact, only one company had a formally posted culture code, and I was one of the team leads that created it. It was helpful. I created one for another company, but the rookie CEO chose never to publish it. Even if a CEO chooses not to publish or discuss a culture code, the company has already organically developed a culture in response to the rookie's PPL.

The process we used for creating a culture code for a company that was already in operation, was to create a survey questionnaire for all employees asking about 20 questions about the company, the vision, the people everyone works with, the CEO, and their individual perspective on what works successfully in the company. In one case, to keep it anonymous, I asked people in the office to place their responses in a manila envelope hanging in the coffee/snack room, and others could send it to me with no names required. There are always a couple of employees who do self-identify, which is fine.

At one company, a senior-level new hire started the survey as he really wanted to hear what people in the company were thinking were strong points, who they thought our customers were, and why there were pockets of significant success. The responses to the survey were enlightening and created a very strong foundation on which to publish the culture code. We then formed a working team to create and execute events and activities that supported the culture.

Why Does It Matter?

Why is a culture code important? It strengthens the environment for employees, partners, customers, and recruiting new employees. For one company, it helped recruit a new leadership team and helped position them for acquisition.

Here are some bullets (not complete) from a culture code just to give you an idea:

- We help our customers and each other.
- We push ourselves to think and be smart.
- We obsess over reliability of systems and people.

- We are remarkable people doing remarkable acts.
- We value data-driven outcomes.

There are some additional benefits from a culture code, which are driven from the PPLC of the rookie CEO or from prior to the rookie appearing on the scene. How the CEO communicates with the employees of all levels, be it open or secretive, is a key part of the culture. Are colleagues encouraged to talk to one another and help each other? How is conflict between competing priorities or departments managed to resolve and move forward? Human nature and caring about one another are key attributes of culture, which can spell success or failure. For future CEOs, think hard about this from day one.

Rookie CEO Story: Stuffed Animals and Real-Time Recognition

Culture includes events for employees, recognition, awards, and anything that is employee-oriented. The following example was intended to engage management teams and employees while providing recognition awards.

This rookie CEO was trying to install new ways to show employee appreciation. This was a good idea. There were stuffed animals, candy bars, stickers, and various other ways to "catch people doing something right." By collecting the stuffed animals from several awards, the employee could trade up to higher value awards. This plan was appreciated, but it was mocked by some of the longer-term executives that had really lost their direction of leadership. I gave this rookie points for attempt and effort, but the execution was not there due to lack of buy-in from several of the senior leadership team. I do think it is a great idea to recognize employees for doing the right thing, doing something above and beyond, and simply being cooperative when the project is not to their benefit specifically.

Think about how you can keep employees involved, cooperative, and always willing to help. One of my early career companies used "night on the town" awards, which were gift cards to a restaurant, cash awards for excellence on projects, and similar simple things. Employees could nominate other employees, which can be powerful.

There was a second stuffed animal example with another rookie CEO, where each conference room had a stuffed animal on the table. If someone started saying things negative, someone else could throw the stuffed animal at the negative person. I can understand the rookie trying to change the culture from a negative one, but throwing stuffed animals was not well-received.

Rookie CEO Story: Seven Dwarfs

In this story, the Cyclone wanted to create fun within the leadership team as part of her ongoing culture change.

Each member of the senior leadership team was to classify each peer as one of the seven dwarfs. Next, imagine the spreadsheet that mapped each of the senior leadership team's classifications is shared among all peers in one meeting, so you can quickly see how everyone classified you. Of course, each dwarf has a definition. For example, there's Doc, who is the leader of the seven dwarfs. Sleepy is the always tired dwarf, and to remind you of the remaining dwarfs: Dopey is accident-prone and the only non-bearded one (different); Bashful is kind-hearted, shy, and cute; Grumpy is not cranky as the name suggests, but opposes things and then changes to help others and to lead; Sneezy is always sneezing, literally blowing papers and things across the room; and finally there's Happy, who is always laughing.

Innuendos were clearly played when the peers mapped each other. If the Cyclone had summarized the chart, made it fun, and did not share every detail, this exercise would and could have been fun and successful. However, as it was presented, all it did was cause conflict among the team. Today, many years later, I have this spreadsheet, and I do have a serious laugh and smile on my face when I read it, all the while thinking to myself, "Bill, you can't make this stuff up!" Transparency is generally good, but in this particular case, it was not a good thing and certainly created a culture of discomfort and resentment among the team—the exact opposite of its intention.

Rookie CEO Story: Ropes, Walls, and Falls

The following example could be placed in the philosophy section, but it was a cultural change this rookie was attempting to drive home to the team. Here's what happened: most rookies try and find ways to build team camaraderie and trust in each other. Coming from a larger company, one rookie CEO chose to do an outdoor team-building retreat for a few days. We went to the hills above Los Angeles to a location built for outdoor team building. We did the trust fall, walked tightropes supporting each other, climbed a 37-foot pole and jumped off, as well as attended several classes, all to learn about each other and build trust. Because this rookie had inherited a senior leadership team that did a lot of passing on the blame, the rookie was hoping this team-building time would encourage everyone to trust each other and work more closely with each other.

It was a first and last for me, and I enjoyed much of it. The overall cost to the company's budget was significant for the senior leadership team, and the payback would be debatable in terms of creating the culture of trust the CEO aimed for. In hindsight, I can see where this exercise could help some teams.

Rookie CEO Story: Office Hours

The following example is from a company whose "stale" culture we were in the process of changing. As a company that provided 24/7 customer support, there were always support people available for calls. Normal office hours were 8 am to 5 pm with other shifts supporting clients.

This rookie CEO started changing their personal office hours to about 9:30 am to 4:30 pm because of drop-off and pickup of their

Disney lllustrate still / not effective

child from daycare as well as going to the gym after drop-off and then arriving at the office where they took a shower before being available for meetings. This same rookie did not like when other office workers on normal hours would come in late or leave early, and reprimanded those workers. As part of the changing culture, the rookie needed to either allow all employees the same flexibility that they took with their own schedule or change their hours back to normal office hours. The management team worked together to agree on what was acceptable for hours in and out of the office for everyone, CEO included. The solution was flexible hours, as long as off-hours and weekends were covered for customer calls.

Lesson to learn: remember rookies, all eyes are on you and your behavior! Behavior matters!

Rookie CEO Story: Back-to-Back CEO Change and Cultural 180

Here, I'm sharing the story mentioned at the chapter's start to show, among other things, how a single CEO can totally determine a company's culture.

The Flyboy was used to meeting new people, many students, and hiring them if he liked them and their customer service style. As mostly lower-level new hires, most of these worked out reasonably well. He had two trusted advisors, both C-suite executives with other companies. One was much older and retired already, and the second was on the board of directors of our company. The Flyboy was driven by investors to hire another senior executive, as I was the only experienced VP and senior person at the time. This outside executive was the second of the Flyboy's trusted advisors, so he came over from the other company as a new rookie CEO. This would be the General. His path was as a successful C-suite executive, but this would be his first CEO role. CEO was a natural progression for him. From day one, the Flyboy gave up control of what he built—from company culture to salary structure to products and services. He still held chairman of the board title, but over time disappeared from day-to-day meetings and decisions. The Flyboy had hired a trusted friend, so he was good with the General taking over completely.

This former C-suite executive, the General, was a seasoned senior leader already. The General as a rookie CEO was by far the most senior-level and most grounded of the new rookie CEOs featured. The General went on to hire several trusted managers, directors, and vice presidents from his former company. In doing so, our company essentially became a mini-version of his former company, which turned the Flyboy's culture upside down. There were new politics that had been nonexistent under the Flyboy. It was very different. Good people were targeted to get driven out of the company because the new managers wanted to replace them with their former colleagues. This kept going on for years. The General managed to bring in a full team of his trusted people around him, allowing him to be the leader he chose to be. For existing executives, it was not a good experience, but it worked well for the General's friends and former colleagues.

Dissecting the takeaways from the Flyboy and the General's rookie CEO experiences, consider what may happen if you are a rookie CEO and you grow your company successfully, take on additional investment money to take the company to the next level, and the investor wants to bring in senior-level experience. There are multiple choices on how to execute this move to make the investor happy. The investor may have a CEO already selected. The investor may choose to bring in a chief operating officer (COO) to keep you as CEO, but your second in command, this COO, would run day-to-day business. In our case, it was the new CEO, the General, that was brought in. When this happens, though, the best way it may work is to transfer leadership and ownership to the new rookie CEO, which the Flyboy did. The results were the changing of culture, the hiring of the General's trusted friends and former colleagues, and the next phase of company growth.

Chapter 9 Takeaways

- Never underestimate the value and impact of the culture that you build or that emerges under your leadership.
- Build a cross-functional culture team and culture code.
- Think about culture from day one in everything that you do.
- Publish your culture code and use it to guide the company, recruit the type of people that fit into your culture, and support your leadership team to execute to your culture code.

CHAPTER 10

Conclusion: For Future CEOs

not me !!

We end this book by looking at some final "you can't make this stuff up!" stories to inform and educate readers. Also we review the overall lessons learned and advice for future rookie CEOs and executives reporting to them. I hope you gather some powerful takeaways for your own rise to CEO leadership or that you gain an informed perspective, should you be working for a rookie CEO.

Rookie CEO Stories: Don't Answer a Question That Is NOT Asked!

The following stories provide a review of my two meeting mantras but apply to any meeting, call, interview, and virtually any life experience. I like to share these mantras with my teams, and I also teach them in coaching sessions.

Imagine this: you are in a meeting, heading toward closing the sale. Everyone is happy. The sales head says, "We have removed all obstacles now, so I assume you are ready to place your order!" The customer responds positively and instructs the sales head to send the final quote with delivery schedules and agreed-upon pricing. All is done! Then one person on your team stands up, getting their coat on, and says to the customer, "I thought you were going to ask about our specific support plan for your remote offices." The customer says, "What? You don't have that? Let's sit back down and take a closer look." Now the deal is unclosed. I watched this happen. You can't make this stuff up!

Here's another related story, starring one of the featured rookie startup CEOs. We had a meeting with a very large company who might have been a potential acquirer somewhere down the line. This was an initial exploratory meeting to educate the visitors at our facility. Our rookie leader loved small talk at the beginning of our meetings all the time, be it a board meeting or customer meeting. This time, as the leaders of the company were sitting, the rookie wondered aloud to them, "Have you looked at how the merging of our two companies might look in the competitive market?" This small talk question that the rookie took it upon themselves to throw out there killed the meeting. The visitors stood up, saying, "We must be in the wrong meeting or misunderstood the agenda," and the meeting was over. You really can't make this stuff up!

About the two above stories: even if it might be a true statement, NEVER answer a question that is not asked or pose a seemingly fun hypothetical question, especially one with such deep tentacles as the one in the second story. Never answer a question that is not asked—is one of my core meeting mantras.

In a similar situation, one rookie had a customer meeting. The team members he chose to bring to the meeting turned out to be a mistake for, as customers asked questions, one of the team members disrupted the rookie's train of thought and disrupted the direction the meeting was intended to go. This team member answered multiple questions that were meant for the rookie CEO. This team member was never invited to a pre-sale meeting again. It could have been a very costly mistake. Think these through for meetings: agenda, top questions you may get, who are best team members to include in the meeting. Do a dry run, if necessary, to ensure no costly mistakes and how the meeting and questions will be managed.

And remember meeting mantra #2: never answer a question that is meant for someone else in the same meeting.

Where Are They Now?

In case you are wondering where our nine rookies are today, let me tell you:

- The Dealmaker is CEO of a successful business he founded going on 18 years now.
- The General is COO of a large successful biotech company.
- The Flyboy is founder, CEO of a second software company.
- The Builder is a venture capitalist and angel investor.
- The Technoid is a technical program manager at a large public company.
- The Cyclone is a social worker in a major US city.
- The Innovatist is CEO of a startup company.
- The Opportunist is a senior executive at the company that acquired his company.
- The Pipeline is retired from technology.

A Rookie's Advice for Future Rookie CEOs

The following advice comes directly from one of our featured rookie CEOs:

1. Respect your executive team.
2. Eliminate if you believe you have the wrong person in the wrong job.

3. Ensure your executive team has everything they need to execute.
4. Ensure that you, as rookie CEO, have a vision, and if anyone does not align, remove them.
5. As rookie CEO, you will have to change your plan.
6. Be aware of new executives brought in by the board of directors; they may be on a mission you don't appreciate.
7. Ensure that executive team members that you invite to board meetings have clear assignments and stay on protocol for the meetings.

8. Plan for the day that the board of directors will replace you, and embrace it.

Final Takeaways

- Learn some strange, powerful, and unique lessons from the stories in this book.
- Every company is different.
- Every leadership team is different.
- As CEO, you own the strategy and direction of the company. Building the right team, at the right time, will contribute to success. Mistakes can be costly, so continue to review and refine on an ongoing basis.
- Plan customer meetings you will be leading, both internal and external.

- Even as a rookie CEO, have a succession plan.

To conclude, readers, let's keep in mind that it's always easy for those that don't have to do it themselves. And, as always, you can't make this stuff up!

ACKNOWLEDGMENTS

A special thanks to Mark Essayian, Rich Tehrani, Anthea Strezze, Chris Nikkel, Rob Leon, Russ Schumacher, and everyone who supported my writing and publishing of the book. I also want to call out the SPS Mastermind Community and Scott Allan who was my writing coach. Without Scott's guidance, this book would never have been completed

ABOUT THE AUTHOR

Bill Miller has been in the technology field for over 40 years. Over the past two decades Bill worked directly for the rookie CEOs featured in this book. His roles reporting to these rookies included Vice President of Marketing, Vice President of Product Management, Vice President of Product Management and Marketing, Vice President of Strategic Planning and Alliance Management, Vice President of Broadband Services, and Vice President of Operations. He has been a blogger for ZDNet, TMCNet, BlogSpot, and for several companies.

Bill has been a speaker at dozens of conferences in networking, VoIP, unified communications, and collaboration markets.

Bill is an executive advisor and consultant, speaker, author, mentor and coach who helps technology company CEOs and leadership with a structured approach to people, process, products and services. As a vice president and leader who has led virtually every major business function in the past 30 years in companies of all sizes from early stage startups to billion-dollar multinational companies, his experience can accelerate your business while guiding and coaching through the most difficult times.

If you are interested in the possibility of working together with me, contact me at bill@billmillertheCEOguy.com.

Bill resides in Connecticut with his fiancée, Connie, and their two dogs and two cats.

- Connect with Bill on LinkedIn: https://www.linkedin.com/in/beelinebill/
- Connect with Bill on Twitter: https://twitter.com/beelinebill

WHAT'S NEXT?

Love this book? Don't forget to leave an honest review!
Every review matters, and it matters a *lot!*
Head over to Amazon or wherever you purchased
this book to leave an honest review for me.

Thank you endlessly.
For any questions, email Bill at bill@billmillertheauthor.com

CPSIA information can be obtained
at www.ICGtesting.com
Printed in the USA
LVHW081321100122
708198LV00003B/17